Benghazi: The Truth The Liberal Media Doesn't Want You To Know

I0447688

The 2012 Benghazi attack refers to a coordinated attack against two US government facilities in Benghazi, Libya by members of the Islamic militant group Ansar al-Sharia in September 2012.

At 9:40 PM, September 11, 2012, members of Ansar al-Sharia attacked the American diplomatic compound in Benghazi resulting in the deaths of U.S. Ambassador to Libya J. Christopher Stevens and U.S. Foreign Service Information Management Officer Sean Smith.

At around 4:00 AM on September 12, the group launched a mortar attack against a CIA annex approximately one mile away, killing CIA contractors Tyrone S. Woods and Glen Doherty and wounding ten others.

At the behest of the CIA, top U.S. officials initially described the attacks as the results of a spontaneous protest triggered by recently released anti-Muslim video, Innocence of Muslims. Subsequent investigations showed that while the attack likely was in retaliation for the video, it was premeditated – although rioters and looters not acting with the group may have later joined in after the attacks begun.

Stevens was the first U.S. Ambassador killed in the line of duty since 1979.

The National Review later labeled the attack Battle of Benghazi, a name that has since been used to refer to the attacks by several media outlets.

There is no definitive evidence that al-Qaeda or any other international terrorist organization participated in the Benghazi attack.

The United States immediately increased security worldwide at diplomatic and military facilities and began investigating the Benghazi attack.

Many Libyans have condemned the attacks. They staged public demonstrations condemning Ansar Al-Sharia, which had been formed during the 2011 Libyan civil war for the purpose of opposing its long-time leader Colonel Muammar Gaddafi).

State Department officials were later criticized for denying requests for additional security at the consulate prior to the attack. In her role as Secretary of State, Hillary Clinton subsequently took responsibility for the security lapses.

Hillary Clinton's actions before, during, and after the attacks have been closely scrutinized by the Republican-led US House of Representatives and by the media, with the topic frequently invoked in the years and months leading up to her 2016 US presidential campaign as a Democrat. Her opponent, Donald Trump, has featured the attacks prominently in his campaign against her.

On August 6, 2013, it was reported that the U.S. had filed criminal charges against several individuals alleged to have been involved in the attacks, including militia leader Ahmed Abu Khattala. Khattala has been described by Libyan and U.S. officials as the Benghazi leader of Ansar al-Sharia. The U.S. Department of State designated Ansar al-Sharia as a terrorist organization in January 2014.

Khattala was captured in Libya by U.S. Army Special Operations Forces, who were acting in coordination with the FBI, in June 2014.

Background

Militants like Abdul Hakeem Belhaj, who fought alongside Al-Qaeda in Afghanistan, other former members of the Libyan Islamic Fighting Group or other radical movements, as well as jihadists who had fought in Iraq and Afghanistan, were essential in the effort to overthrow Gadhafi. That spring, weapons began being shipped to rebels through Qatar with American approval. By September 2011, Western counterterrorism officials had become increasingly concerned with the role Islamic radicals were playing in the revolt in Libya, and worried the weapons acquired by them during the war would be used in future terrorist attacks.

Within months of the start of the Libyan revolution in February 2011, the CIA began building a covert presence in Benghazi. During the war, elite counterterrorist operators from America's Delta Force were deployed to Libya as analysts, instructing the rebels on specifics about weapons and tactics.:16 Ambassador J. Christopher Stevens was named the first liaison with the Libyan opposition in March 2011. After the end of the war, both the CIA and the U.S. State Department were tasked with continuing to identify and collect arms that had flooded the country during the war, particularly shoulder-fired missiles taken from the arsenal of the Gaddafi regime, as well as securing Libyan chemical weapons stockpiles, and helping to train Libya's new intelligence service.

Eastern Libya and Benghazi were key intelligence-gathering hubs for intelligence operatives. Before the attack, the CIA was monitoring Ansar al-Sharia and suspected members of Al-Qaeda in the Islamic Maghreb, as well as attempting to define the leadership and loyalty of the various militias present and their interaction with the Salafi elements of Libyan society. By the time of the attack, dozens of CIA operatives were on the ground in Benghazi. In addition, it has been reported that in the summer of 2012, American Joint Special Operations Command (JSOC) missions had begun to target Libyan militias linked to the Al-Qaeda network of Yasin al-Suri.:58 By the time of the attack, a composite U.S. Special Operations team with two JSOC members was already in Libya working on their mission profile independently of the CIA and State Department operations.:58

Multiple anonymous sources reported that the diplomatic mission in Benghazi was used by the CIA as a cover to smuggle weapons from Libya to anti-Assad rebels in Syria.:56 Investigative journalist Seymour Hersh cites an anonymous former senior Defense

Department intelligence official, saying "The consulate's only mission was to provide cover for the moving of arms. It had no real political role." The attack allegedly brought an end to the purported U.S. involvement, but did not stop the smuggling according to Hersh's source. In January 2014, the House Permanent Select Committee on Intelligence cast doubt on this alleged U.S. involvement and reported that "All CIA activities in Benghazi were legal and authorized. On-the-record testimony establishes that the CIA was not sending weapons ... from Libya to Syria, or facilitating other organizations or states that were transferring weapons from Libya to Syria."

During Congressional hearings, Ambassador Stevens' top deputy in Libya, Gregory N. Hicks, testified that Ambassador Stevens was in Benghazi in 2012 because "Secretary Clinton wanted the post made permanent", and it was understood that the secretary hoped to make an announcement to that effect during a visit to Tripoli later in the year. He also stated that "Chris wanted to make a symbolic gesture to the people of Benghazi that the United States stood behind their dream of establishing a new democracy."

In April 2012, two former security guards for the consulate threw an IED over the consulate fence; the incident did not cause any casualties. Just four days later, a similar bomb was thrown at a four-vehicle convoy carrying the United Nations Special Envoy to Libya, exploding twelve feet from the UN envoy's vehicle without injuring anyone.

In May 2012, an Al-Qaida affiliate calling itself the "Brigades of the Imprisoned Sheikh Omar Abdul Rahman" claimed responsibility for an attack on the International Red Cross (ICRC) office in Benghazi. On August 6, the ICRC suspended operations in Benghazi. The head of the ICRC's delegation in Libya said the aid group was "appalled" by the attack and "extremely concerned" about escalating violence in Libya.

The Brigades of the Imprisoned Sheikh Omar Abdul Rahman released a video of what it said was its detonation of an explosive device outside the gates of the U.S. consulate on June 6, which caused no casualties but blew a hole in the consulate's perimeter wall, described by one individual as "big enough for forty men to go through". The Brigades claimed that the attack was in response to the killing of Abu

Yahya al Libi, a Libyan al-Qaeda leader who had just died in an American drone attack, and was also timed to coincide with the imminent arrival of a U.S. diplomat. There were no injuries, but the group left behind leaflets promising more attacks against the U.S.

British ambassador to Libya Dominic Asquith survived an assassination attempt in Benghazi on June 10. Two British protection officers were injured in the attack when their convoy was hit by a rocket-propelled grenade 300 yards from their consulate office. The British Foreign Office withdrew all consular staff from Benghazi in late June.

On June 18, 2012, the Tunisian consulate in Benghazi was attacked by individuals affiliated with Ansar al-Sharia, allegedly because of "attacks by Tunisian artists against Islam".:31

On the day of the attack, two consulate security guards spotted a man in a Libyan police uniform taking pictures of the consulate with his cell phone from a nearby building that was under construction. The security guards briefly detained the man before releasing him. He drove away in a police car and a complaint was made to the Libyan police station. Sean Smith noticed this surveillance, and messaged a friend online around noon, "Assuming we don't die tonight. We saw one of our 'police' that guard the compound taking pictures.":34

According to a local security official, he and a battalion commander had met with U.S. diplomats three days before the attack and warned the Americans about deteriorating security in the area. The official told CNN that he advised the diplomats, "The situation is frightening; it scares us."

Ambassador Stevens' diary, which was later found at the compound, recorded his concern about the growing al-Qaeda presence in the area and his worry about being on an al-Qaeda hit list.

U.S. security officer Eric Nordstrom twice requested additional security for the mission in Benghazi from the State Department. His requests were denied and according to Nordstrom, State Department official Charlene Lamb wanted to keep the security presence in Benghazi "artificially low".

On December 30, 2012, the United States Senate Committee on Homeland Security and Governmental Affairs released a report, "Flashing Red: A Special Report on the Terrorist Attack at Benghazi", wherein it was determined:

The desire of the State Department to maintain a low profile in Benghazi has been cited as the reason why the State Department circumvented their own Overseas Security Policy Board (OSPB) standards for diplomatic security.:74–75 In the aftermath, Clinton sought to take responsibility for the security lapses at Benghazi and expressed personal regret. In her January 2013 testimony before Congress, Secretary Clinton claimed security decisions at the Benghazi compound had been made by others, stating, "The specific security requests pertaining to Benghazi ... were handled by the security professionals in the Department. I didn't see those requests, I didn't approve them, I didn't deny them."

Attack

The Benghazi attack consisted of military assaults on two separate U.S. compounds. The first assault occurred at the main diplomatic compound, approximately 300 yards long and 100 yards wide, at about 9:40 p.m. local time (3:40 p.m. Eastern Time). A mortar fire attack on a CIA annex 1.2 miles away (coordinates 32°03′26″N 20°05′16″E / 32.0572°N 20.0877°E / 32.0572; 20.0877 (CIA annex)) began at about 4:00 a.m. the following morning and lasted for 11 minutes.

Between 125 and 150 gunmen, "some wearing the Afghan-style tunics favored by Islamic militants", are reported to have participated in the assault. Some of the assailants had their faces covered and wore flak jackets. Weapons they used during the attack included rocket-propelled grenades (RPGs), hand grenades, AK-47 and FN F2000 assault rifles, diesel canisters, mortars, and heavy machine guns and artillery mounted on gun trucks.

The assault began at nightfall, with the attackers sealing off streets leading to the main compound with gun trucks. The trucks bore the logo of Ansar al-Sharia, a group of Islamist militants working with the local government to manage security in Benghazi. (Ansar al-Sharia was listed in January 2014 by the U.S. Department of State as a terrorist organization.)

One Libyan guard who was wounded in the attack was quoted as saying "there wasn't a single ant outside ." The attackers stated they were acting in response to Innocence of Muslims. No more than seven Americans were in the compound, including Ambassador Stevens.

Stevens was visiting Benghazi at the time to review plans to establish a new cultural center and modernize a hospital. The ambassador also "needed to report ... on the physical and the political and security environment in Benghazi to support an action memo to convert Benghazi from a temporary facility to a permanent facility". Surplus funds originally dedicated for use in Iran for fiscal year 2012 were to be redirected and obligated for use in Benghazi: an action that had to be completed before the end of the fiscal year—September 30, 2012.

Stevens had his last meeting of the day with a Turkish diplomat, and escorted the Turkish diplomat to the main gate at about 8:30 p.m. local time. The street outside the compound was calm, and the State Department reported no unusual activity during the day outside. Stevens retired to his room at about 9:00 p.m.

About 9:40 p.m. local time, large numbers of armed men shouting "Allāhu Akbar" (God is great) approached the compound from multiple directions. They then threw grenades over the wall and entered the compound with automatic weapons fire, RPGs, and heavier weapons. A Diplomatic Security Service (DSS) agent viewed on the consulate's security cameras "a large number of men, armed men, flowing into the compound". He hit the alarm and started shouting, "Attack! Attack!" over the loudspeaker. Phone calls were made to the embassy in Tripoli, the Diplomatic Security Command Center in Washington, the February 17th Martyrs Brigade and a U.S. quick reaction force located at the annex compound a little more than a mile away. Ambassador Stevens telephoned Deputy Chief of Mission Gregory Hicks in Tripoli to tell him the consulate was under attack. Hicks did not recognize the phone number so he did not answer it, twice. On the third call Hicks answered the call.

Diplomatic Security Service Special Agent Scott Strickland secured Stevens and Sean Smith, an information management officer, in the main building's safe haven. The rest of the agents left to retrieve their weapons and tried to return to the main building. The attackers entered the main building and attempted to enter the safe haven. They then spread the diesel fuel in the room and set fires. Stevens, Smith, and Strickland moved to the nearby bathroom, but then decided to leave the safe haven after being overcome by smoke. Strickland exited through the window, but Stevens and Smith did not follow him. Strickland returned several times but could not find them in the smoke; he went up to the roof and radioed other agents. Three agents returned to the main building in an armored vehicle, searched the building and found Smith's body, but not Stevens.

According to the Annex Security Team, they had become a,ware of the consulate attack after 9:30 p.m. local time, and were ready to respond; however, they were delayed by "the top CIA officer in Benghazi". The Regional Security Office sounded the alarm and called to the Benghazi CIA annex and the embassy in Tripoli. After some discussion, the CIA's Global Response Staff (GRS) at the CIA annex, which included Tyrone S. Woods, decided to attempt a rescue. By 10:05 p.m., the team was briefed and loaded into their armored Toyota Land Cruisers. By this time, communicators at the CIA annex were notifying the chain of command about current developments, and a small CIA and JSOC element in Tripoli that included Glen Doherty was attempting to find a way to Benghazi.:39–43

The GRS team from the CIA annex arrived at the consulate and attempted to secure the perimeter and locate the ambassador and Sean Smith. Diplomatic security agent David Ubben located Smith, who was unconscious and later declared dead, but the team was unable to find Stevens in the smoke-filled building. The team then decided to return to the annex with the survivors and Smith's body. While en route back to the annex, the group's armored vehicle was hit by AK-47 rifle fire and hand grenades. The vehicle was able to make it to its destination with two flat tires, and the gates to the annex were closed behind them at 11:50 p.m.:43–45

Abdel-Monem Al-Hurr, the spokesman for Libya's Supreme Security Committee, said roads leading to the Benghazi consulate compound were sealed off and Libyan state security forces had surrounded it.

A U.S. Army commando unit was sent to Naval Air Station Sigonella in Sicily, Italy the night of the attack but did not deploy to Benghazi. U.S. officials say the team did not arrive at Sigonella until after the attack was over.

Diplomatic Security Service agents/Regional Security Officers informed their headquarters in Washington about the attack just as it was beginning at about 9:40 local time (3:40 p.m. Eastern Time (ET)). At the time, they were informed that the attack was a "terrorist attack". By 4:30 p.m. ET, Pentagon officials had informed Defense Secretary Leon Panetta about the attack. The Pentagon ordered an unmanned aerial vehicle that was in the air conducting surveillance on militant camps to fly over Benghazi. The drone arrived at 11:10 p.m. local time (5:10 p.m. ET) and began providing a video feed to Washington. At 5:41 p.m. ET, Secretary of State Hillary Clinton telephoned CIA Director David Petraeus to coordinate. The CIA, which made up most of the U.S. government's presence in Benghazi, had a ten-member security team at its annex and the State Department believed that this team would assist the consulate in the event of an attack.

Just after midnight, the CIA annex came under machine gun, rocket and mortar fire. The CIA defenders held off the attack until the morning.:45–46 That same morning, Libyan government forces met up with a group of Americans, reinforcements from Tripoli including Glen Doherty, that had arrived at the Benghazi airport. The team, which included two active-duty JSOC operators and five CIA personnel, had commandeered a small jet in Tripoli by paying the pilots $30,000 and forcing them to fly to Benghazi.:43 After being held up at the airport for a few hours, the Libyan forces and newly arrived Americans went to the CIA annex at about 5:00 a.m. to assist in transporting approximately 32 Americans at the annex back to the airport for evacuation. Minutes after they drove through the gates, the annex came under heavy fire. With a lull in the fighting, Doherty began searching for his friend, Tyrone S. Woods, and he was told he was on the roof. He found Woods on the roof with two other agents. A mortar round then hit Woods' position, fatally wounding him. As Doherty attempted to reposition and take cover, a second round fell on him, killing him.:46–47 31-year-old Diplomatic Security Service Special Agent David Ubben suffered shrapnel injuries and several broken bones in the mortar attacks.

Immediately, several agents ran onto the roof to assess damage and help the wounded. At the same time, a JSOC operator was using a hand-held device displaying images from a Predator drone above, which had been sent by the DOD's Africa Command after request. The defenders agreed to evacuate to the airport and were attacked with small arms fire along the route.:47–48 The evacuation of about 30 Americans included six State Department personnel and Smith's body—they were unable to locate Ambassador Stevens at the time.

Ambassador Stevens' body was found by a group of Libyans who had accessed the room through a window. They were unaware of his identity; and Abdel-Qader Fadl, a freelance photographer who was with them, told the Associated Press that Stevens was unconscious and "maybe moved his head, but only once". Ahmed Shams, a 22-year-old arts student, told the Associated Press that they were happy when they found Stevens alive and tried to rescue him. A freelance videographer, Fahd al-Bakoush, later published a video showing Libyans trying to extract the ambassador from a smoke-filled room, where he was found unconscious. According to al-Bakoush, the Libyans saw he was alive and breathing, his eyelids flickering. Though they took him to be a foreigner, no one recognized him as Stevens.

At around 1:00 am, Stevens was taken to the Benghazi Medical Center, a hospital controlled by the Ansar Al-Sharia militia, in a private car as there was no ambulance to carry him. There he was administered CPR for 90 minutes by Dr. Ziad Abu Zeid. According to Dr. Zeid, Stevens died from asphyxiation caused by smoke inhalation, and had no other apparent injuries. The doctor said he believed that officers from the Libyan Interior Ministry transported the body to the airport. State Department officials said they do not know who took Stevens to the hospital or transported the body to the airport and into U.S. custody.

The bodies were taken to Benina International Airport and flown to the capital, Tripoli, and then to Ramstein Air Base in Germany aboard a C-17 military transport aircraft. From Germany, the four bodies arrived at Andrews Air Force Base near Washington, D.C., where President Barack Obama and members of his cabinet held a ceremony in honor of those killed.

After the attack, all diplomatic staff were moved to the capital, Tripoli, with nonessential personnel to be flown out of Libya. Sensitive documents remained missing, including documents listing the names of Libyans working with the Americans, and documents relating to oil contracts.

Four Americans died in the attack: Ambassador J. Christopher Stevens, Information Officer Sean Smith, and two CIA operatives, Glen Doherty and Tyrone Woods, both former Navy SEALs. Stevens was the first U.S. ambassador killed in an attack since Adolph Dubs was killed in Kabul, Afghanistan in 1979.

On September 10, 2012, at least 18 hours before the attack in Benghazi, al-Qaeda leader Ayman al-Zawahiri released a video to coincide with the anniversary of the 9/11 attacks in 2001, which called for attacks on Americans in Libya in order to avenge the death of Abu Yahya al-Libi in a drone strike in Pakistan in June 2012. It is uncertain how much prior knowledge of the attack al-Zawahiri had, though he praised the attackers on October 12, 2012 in another video. On September 14, 2012, al-Qaeda in the Arabian Peninsula released a statement arguing the attack was revenge for the death of al-Libi, though they did not claim official responsibility for the Benghazi attack. It was later reported that 3 operatives from the group did take part in the attack. Further, an intercepted phone call from the Benghazi area immediately after the attack reportedly linked senior Al-Qaeda in the Islamic Maghreb commander Mokhtar Belmokhtar to the attack.

David Kirkpatrick of The New York Times reported that 20-year-old neighbor Mohamed Bishari witnessed the attack. According to Bishari, it was launched without warning or protest and was led by the Islamist militia Ansar al-Sharia (different from the group called Ansar al-Sharia based in Yemen designated by the U.N. and the U.S. Department of State as a terrorist organization). Kirkpatrick reported that Ansar al-Sharia said they were launching the assault in retaliation for the release of the anti-Islamic video, Innocence of

Muslims. It was further reported that Ahmed Abu Khattala was called a ringleader of the attack by both witnesses and authorities, though he insisted he did not play a part in the aggression at the American compound. Witnesses, Benghazi residents, and Western news reports have described him as a leader of Ansar al-Sharia, though he stated he was close to the group but not an official part of it. He further stated he was the commander of an Islamist brigade, Abu Obaida ibn al-Jarrah, some of whose members had joined Ansar al-Sharia.

The Brigades of the Imprisoned Sheikh Omar Abdul Rahman, a pro-al-Qaeda militia calling for the release of The Blind Sheik, was implicated in the attack by Noman Benotman of the Quilliam Foundation. CNN, the Carnegie Endowment for International Peace, Commentary Magazine and The Daily Telegraph have listed this group as a chief suspect. USA Today reported that protests in Cairo that preceded the attack on Benghazi were intended to protest the imprisonment of Sheik Omar Abdul Rahman and announced as early as August 30. Egyptian President Mohammed Morsi had called for release of the Blind Sheikh in his inaugural address.

In the days and weeks following the attack, President Obama and other administration officials noted that the video had sparked violent incidents at a number of U.S. diplomatic facilities and stated it was also a prime catalyst for the Benghazi attack. On the evening following the attack, in an e-mail to the Egyptian prime minister Kandil, then Secretary of State Hillary Clinton wrote "we know the attack in Libya had nothing to do with the film. It was a planned attack, not a protest." Two days after the attack, CNN reporter Sarah Aarthun quoted an anonymous senior U.S. administration official: "It was not an innocent mob. The video or 9/11 made a handy excuse and could be fortuitous from their perspective but this was a clearly planned military-type attack." In his September 18 appearance on the Late Show with David Letterman, President Obama said, "extremists and terrorists used (the anti-Muslim YouTube video) as an excuse to attack a variety of our embassies." In his Univision Town Hall appearance on September 20, President Obama said that the "natural protests that arose because of the outrage over the video were used as an excuse by extremists to see if they can also directly harm U.S. interests." A later report from an independent review board concluded "there was no protest prior to the attacks."

In October 2012, a Tunisian Ali Harzi, who a U.S. intelligence official stated had links to Ansar al-Sharia and al-Qaeda in the Maghreb, was arrested in Turkey and repatriated to Tunisia on terrorism charges and possible links to the attack on the U.S. consulate in Benghazi. Ali Harzi was released by Tunisian authorities on January 8, 2013 because of a lack of evidence.

Also in October, a Libyan suspect, Karim el-Azizi, who had recently returned to Egypt from Libya and was storing weapons in his hideout, detonated a bomb and was found dead in his apartment after clashes with security forces. He has been linked to an Egyptian terrorist group led by Muhammad Jamal Abu Ahmad, who is suspected of training some of the terrorists responsible for the Benghazi attack in camps in the Libyan desert. Jamal Abu Ahmad, a former member of Egyptian Islamic Jihad, was released from Egyptian prison after the fall of the Mubarak regime, after which he began assembling a terrorist network. He received financing from the Yemen-based Al-Qaeda in the Arabian Peninsula, petitioned Al-Qaeda leader Ayman al-Zawahiri to establish a new Al-Qaeda affiliate he called al-Qaeda in Egypt, and was subsequently detained by Egyptian authorities in December 2012. On October 7, 2013, the Muhammad Jamal network

(MJN) and Muhammad Jamal were designated as "global terrorists" by the U.S. Department of State. The U.S. State Department noted in its designation that Jamal "has developed connections with al-Qa'ida in the Islamic Maghreb (AQIM), AQ senior leadership, and al-Qa'ida in the Arabian Peninsula (AQAP) leadership including Nasir 'Abd-al-Karim 'Abdullah al-Wahishi and Qasim Yahya Mahdi al-Rimi". A few days later, on October 21, 2013, the United Nations Security Council designated the MJN "as being associated with Al-Qaida". The United Nations Security Council also noted, "Some of the attackers of the U.S. Mission in Benghazi on September 11, 2012, have been identified as associates of Muhammad Jamal, and some of the Benghazi attackers reportedly trained at MJN camps in Libya."

In March 2013, Faraj al-Shibli was detained by Libyan authorities and questioned by the FBI because of his suspected involvement in the Benghazi attack. Al-Shibli was detained after he returned from a trip to Pakistan, though his exact role in the attack is unclear. He was a member of the Libyan Islamic Fighting Group, which tried to overthrow the Gadhafi regime in the mid-1990s. Investigators have learned he has had contact with both the Yemen-based Al-Qaeda in the Arabian Peninsula and Al-Qaeda members in Pakistan. He was released by Libyan authorities on June 12, 2013, based on claims there was a lack of evidence to hold him in custody. In July 2014 he was found dead in Libya.

Aftermath

Libyan Prime Minister Mustafa Abushagur's office condemned the attack and extended condolences, saying: "While strongly condemning any attempt to abuse the person of Muhammad, or an insult to our holy places and prejudice against the faith, we reject and strongly condemn the use of force to terrorize innocent people and the killing of innocent people." It also reaffirmed "the depth of relationship between the peoples of Libya and the U.S., which grew closer with the positions taken by the U.S. government in support of the revolution of February 17". Mohamed Yousef el-Magariaf, the President of the General National Congress of Libya, said: "We apologise to the United States, the people and to the whole world for what happened. We confirm that no-one will escape from punishment and questioning."

There were demonstrations in Benghazi and Tripoli on September 12, condemning the violence and holding signs such as "Chris Stevens was a friend to all Libyans", "Benghazi is against terrorism", and other signs apologizing to Americans for the actions in their name and in the name of Muslims. On the same day, Libya's Deputy Ambassador to London Ahmad Jibril told the BBC that Ansar Al-Sharia was behind the attack. On September 13, at a U.S. State Department reception in Washington D.C., the Libyan ambassador to the U.S. Ali Aujali apologized to Secretary of State Clinton for "this terrorist attack which took place against the American consulate in Libya". The ambassador further praised Stevens as a "dear friend" and a "real hero". He also urged the United States to continue supporting Libya as it went "through a very difficult time" and that the young Libyan government needed help so that it could "maintain ... security and stability in our country".

In the days after the attack, The New York Times stated that young Libyans had flooded Twitter with pro-American messages after the attacks. Think Progress stated that Libyans are typically more positively inclined towards the United States than their neighbors. A 2012 Gallup poll noted that "A majority of Libyans (54%) surveyed in March and April 2012 approve of the leadership of the U.S.—among the highest approval Gallup has ever recorded in the ... region, outside of Israel." Another poll in Eastern Libya, taken in 2011, reported that the population was at the same time both deeply religious conservative Muslims and very pro-American, with 90% of respondents reporting favorable views of the United States.

The Libyan response to the crisis was praised and appreciated in the United States, and President Obama emphasized how the Libyans "helped our diplomats to safety" to an American audience the following day, while a New York Times editorial criticized Egypt's government for not doing "what Libyan leaders did".

On September 16, Libyan President Mohamed Magariaf said that the attack on the U.S. consulate was planned months in advance, and further stated that "he idea that this criminal and cowardly act was a spontaneous protest that just spun out of control is completely unfounded and preposterous. We firmly believe that this was a precalculated, preplanned attack that was carried out specifically to attack the U.S. consulate."

On September 21, about 30,000 Libyans marched through Benghazi calling for support of the rule of law and for an end to the armed militias that had formed during the Libyan Civil War to oppose

Colonel Gaddafi. After that war, the militias failed to disband, and continually menaced the Libyan government and populace. Carrying signs with slogans such as "We Want Justice For Chris" and "Libya Lost a Friend", the protestors stormed several militia headquarters, including that of Ansar al-Sharia, an Islamist militia who some allege played a role in the attack on U.S. diplomatic personnel on September 11. At least 10 people were killed and dozens more wounded as militiamen fired on demonstrators at the headquarters of Sahaty Brigade, a pro-government militia "operating under the authority of the ministry of defence".

By early next morning, the protestors had forced militia members to flee and seized control of a number of compounds, releasing four prisoners found inside. Protesters burnt a car and a building of at least one facility, and looted weapons. The militia compounds and many weapons were handed over to Libya's national army in what "appeared to be part of a coordinated sweep of militia bases by police, government troops and activists" following the earlier demonstrations. Some militia members accused the protestors of being Gaddafi loyalists, looking to disarm the militias in the wake of the revolution.

On September 23, taking advantage of the growing momentum and rising anger against the militias evinced in the earlier anti-militia demonstrations, the Libyan president declared that all unauthorized militias had 48 hours to either disband or come under government control. The government also mandated that bearing arms in public was now illegal, as were armed checkpoints.

It has been noted that previously, handling the militias had been difficult as the government had been forced to rely on some of them for protection and security. According to a Libyan interviewed in Tripoli, the government gained the ability to push back against the militias because of a "mandate of the people".

On the 24th, the government commenced with a raid on a former military base held by a rogue infantry militia.

Across the country, militias began surrendering to the government. The government formed a "National Mobile Force" for the purpose of evicting illegal militias. On the same day as the declaration, various militias in Misrata held meetings, ultimately deciding to submit to the government's authority, and handed over various public facilities they had been holding, including the city's three main jails, which were handed over to the authority of the Ministry of Justice. Hours before the announcement, in Derna, the two main militias (one of them Ansar al-Sharia) active in the city both withdrew, leaving both their five military bases behind.

Hundreds of Libyans, mainly former rebel fighters, gathered in the city centers of Tripoli and Benghazi to hand over their weapons to the government on September 29.

The campaign has been less successful in other areas, such as the remote Nafusa Mountains, inhabited by the Nafusi-speaking Berber minority, where the Emirati news agency The National reported on September 23 that arms were being hoarded. The National also reported arms being hoarded in Misrata, despite simultaneous reporting by other outlets that militias were surrendering in Misrata.

On September 12, U.S. President Barack Obama condemned "this outrageous attack" on U.S. diplomatic facilities and stated that "since our founding, the United States has been a nation that respects all faiths. We reject all efforts to denigrate the religious beliefs of others." After referring to "the 9/11 attacks", "troops who made the ultimate sacrifice in Iraq and Afghanistan", and "then last night, we learned the news of this attack in Benghazi" the President urged, "As Americans, let us never, ever forget that our freedom is only sustained because there are people who are willing to fight for it, to stand up for it, and in some cases, lay down their lives for it." He then went on to say, "No acts of terror will ever shake the resolve of this great nation, alter that character, or eclipse the light of the values that we stand for. Today we mourn four more Americans who represent the very best of the United States of America. We will not waver in our commitment to see that justice is done for this terrible act. And make no mistake, justice will be done".

After the attack, Obama ordered that security be increased at all such facilities worldwide. A 50-member Marine FAST team was sent to Libya to "bolster security". It was announced that the FBI would investigate the possibility of the attack being planned. U.S. officials said surveillance over Libya would increase, including the use of unmanned drones, to "hunt for the attackers".

Secretary of State Clinton also made a statement on September 12, describing the perpetrators as "heavily armed militants" and "a small and savage group—not the people or government of Libya". She also reaffirmed "America's commitment to religious tolerance" and said "Some have sought to justify this vicious behavior, along with the protest that took place at our Embassy in Cairo yesterday, as a response to inflammatory material posted on the Internet," but whether true or not, that was not a justification for violence. The State Department had previously identified embassy and personnel security as a major challenge in its budget and priorities report.

On September 12, it was reported that the United States Navy dispatched two Arleigh Burke class destroyers, the USS McFaul and the USS Laboon, to the Libyan coast. The destroyers are equipped with Tomahawk cruise missiles. American UAVs were also sent to fly over Libya to search for the perpetrators of the attack.

In a speech on September 13, in Golden, Colorado, President Obama paid tribute to the four Americans "killed in an attack on our diplomatic post in Libya", stating, "We enjoy our security and our liberty because of the sacrifices they make ... I want people around the world to hear me: To all those who would do us harm, no act of terror will go unpunished. It will not dim the light of the values that we proudly present to the rest of the world."

In his press briefing on September 14, White House Press Secretary Jay Carney told reporters that "we don't have and did not have concrete evidence to suggest that this was not in reaction to the film." He went on to say: "There was no intelligence that in any way could have been acted on to prevent these attacks. It is—I mean, I think the DNI spokesman was very declarative about this that the report is false. The report suggested that there was intelligence that was available prior to this that led us to believe that this facility would be attacked, and that is false ... We have no information to suggest that it was a preplanned attack. The unrest we've seen around the region has been in reaction to a video that Muslims, many Muslims find offensive. And while the violence is reprehensible and unjustified, it is not a reaction to the 9/11 anniversary that we know of, or to U.S. policy."

On September 14, the remains of the slain Americans were returned to the U.S., President Obama and Secretary of State Hillary Clinton attended the ceremony. In her remarks Clinton said, "One young woman, her head covered and her eyes haunted with sadness, held up a handwritten sign that said 'Thugs and killers don't represent Benghazi nor Islam.' The President of the Palestinian Authority, who worked closely with Chris when he served in Jerusalem, sent me a letter remembering his energy and integrity, and deploring—and I quote—'an act of ugly terror.'" She went on to say: "We've seen the heavy assault on our post in Benghazi that took the lives of those brave men."

On September 16, the U.S. Ambassador to the U.N. Susan Rice appeared on five major interview shows to discuss the attacks. Prior to her appearance, Rice was provided with "talking points" from a CIA memo, which stated:

Using these talking points as a guide, Rice stated:

In a White House press briefing on September 18, press secretary Jay Carney explained the attack to reporters: "I'm saying that based on information that we—our initial information, and that includes all information—we saw no evidence to back up claims by others that this was a preplanned or premeditated attack; that we saw evidence that it was sparked by the reaction to this video. And that is what we know thus far based on the evidence, concrete evidence."

On September 20, White House Press Secretary Jay Carney answered a question about an open hearing with the National Counterterrorism

Center Director, Matthew G. Olsen, which referenced which extremist groups might have been involved. Carney said, "It is, I think, self-evident that what happened in Benghazi was a terrorist attack. Our embassy was attacked violently, and the result was four deaths of American officials. So, again, that's self-evident." On the same day, during an appearance on Univision, a Spanish-language television network in the United States, President Obama stated, "What we do know is that the natural protests that arose because of the outrage over the video were used as an excuse by extremists to see if they can also directly harm U.S. interests."

Also on September 20, Secretary of State Hillary Clinton gave a classified briefing to U.S. Senators, which several Republican attendees criticized. According to the article, senators were angered at the Obama administration's rebuff of their attempts to learn details of the Benghazi attack, only to see that information published the next day in The New York Times and The Wall Street Journal.

On September 24, advertisements condemning an anti-Islam video appeared on Pakistani television. The television ads in Pakistan (marked with the U.S. Embassy seal) feature clips of President

Obama and Secretary of State Clinton during press appearances in Washington in which they condemned the video. Their words were subtitled in Urdu.

On September 25, in an address before the United Nations General Assembly President Obama stated, "The attacks on our civilians in Benghazi were attacks on America ... And there should be no doubt that we will be relentless in tracking down the killers and bringing them to justice." He referred to Innocence of Muslims as "a crude and disgusting video sparked outrage throughout the Muslim world". He said, "I have made it clear that the United States government had nothing to do with this video, and I believe its message must be rejected by all who respect our common humanity." He further stated, "There is no video that justifies an attack on an Embassy."

On September 26, Clinton acknowledged a possible link between Al-Qaeda in the Islamic Maghreb and the Benghazi attack.

On September 28, a spokesman for the Director of National Intelligence stated "In the immediate aftermath, there was information that led us to assess that the attack began spontaneously following protests earlier that day at our embassy in Cairo. We provided that initial assessment to Executive Branch officials and members of Congress ... As we learned more about the attack, we revised our initial assessment to reflect new information indicating that it was a deliberate and organized terrorist attack carried out by extremists. It remains unclear if any group or person exercised overall command and control of the attack, and if extremist group leaders directed their members to participate." Also on September 28, it was reported that Nakoula Basseley Nakoula, the producer of the Innocence of Muslims video, had been arrested in California and was being held without bail for alleged probation violations stemming from a 2010 bank fraud conviction.

On CNN's State of the Union with Candy Crowley on September 30, Crowley observed that "Friday we got the administration's sort of definitive statement that this now looks as though it was a pre-planned attack by a terrorist group, some of whom were at least sympathetic to al Qaeda," and asked the senior Republican on the Senate Armed Services Committee, Senator John McCain, "why do you think and are you bothered that it has taken them this long from September 11th to now to get to this conclusion?" to which McCain replied that "it interferes with the depiction that the administration is trying to convey that al Qaeda is on the wane ... how else could you trot out our U.N. ambassador to say this was a spontaneous demonstration? ... It was either willful ignorance or abysmal intelligence to think that people come to spontaneous demonstrations with heavy weapons, mortars, and the attack goes on for hours."

On October 4, 22 days after the attack, FBI investigators were finally allowed access to the scene of the attack. The crime scene was not secured during that time; neither American nor Libyan investigators were able to secure the scene. The hearing testimony revealed that "Hicks argued that Rice's comments so insulted the Libyan president—since they contradicted his Sept. 16 claims that the attack was premeditated—that it slowed the FBI's investigation. 'President Magariaf was insulted in front of his own people, in front of the world. His credibility was reduced,' Hicks said, adding that the president was apparently 'still steamed' two weeks later."

To assist the Libyan government in disbanding extremist groups, the Obama administration allocated $8 million to begin building an elite Libyan commando force over the next year.

In the Presidential debate of October 16, 2012, between President Obama and Mitt Romney, Romney claimed that "it took the president 14 days before he called the attack in Benghazi an act of terror." President Obama responded, "The day after the attack, governor, I stood in the Rose Garden and I told the American people and the world that we are going to find out exactly what happened," Obama said. "That this was an act of terror, and I also said that we're going to hunt down those who committed this crime." When Romney challenged Obama, asking "You said in the Rose Garden the day after the attack, it was an act of terror. It was not a spontaneous demonstration, is that what you're saying?" the President responded, "Please proceed, governor" and "Get the transcript." The moderator of the debate, Candy Crowley, agreed, stating "He—he did call it an act of terror." A CNN analysis stated that Obama had indeed referred to the incident as a "terrorist attack", but that Romney was correct in noting that the administration delayed in conclusively stating that the attack was not a spontaneous protest related to the video. A 14 May 2013 Fact Checker by Glenn Kesler said that Obama repeatedly used the phrase "act of terror" when talking about the attack, but he did not directly state that the attack was an act of terror.

On October 19, 2012, House Oversight Committee Chairman Darrell Issa (R-CA) came under fire from intelligence officials in the Obama administration when he posted, on a public website, 166 pages of sensitive but unclassified State Department communications related to Libya. According to officials, the release of the unredacted documents compromised the identities of several Libyans working with the U.S. government and placed their lives in danger.

On CBS's Face the Nation on October 28, Senator John McCain (R-AZ) stated that "this is either a massive cover-up or incompetence" and suggested that it was a scandal worse than Watergate. McCain stated, "we know that there were tapes, recordings inside the consulate during this fight ... So the president went on various shows, despite what he said in the Rose Garden, about terrorist acts, he went on several programs, including The View, including Letterman, including before the UN where he continued to refer, days later, many days later, to this as a spontaneous demonstration because of a hateful video. We know that is patently false. What did the president know? When did he know it? And what did he do about it?" CBS News reported earlier on October 24 that the video of the assault was recovered 20 days after the attack, from the more than 10 security cameras at the compound. In a radio interview October 29, 2012, Senator John McCain said that the surveillance tapes had been classified top secret.

Secretary Clinton was scheduled to testify before Congress on December 20 about the attack. On December 15, it was reported that she had become dehydrated from the flu, fainted, and sustained a concussion. Consequently, her testimony was postponed. The incident prompted Republican Rep. Allen West to claim that the illness was a ruse intended to avoid testifying. Former UN Ambassador John Bolton called the concussion a "diplomatic illness".

On January 23, 2013, during testimony at a Senate hearing on Benghazi, Clinton engaged in a heated exchange with Senator Ron Johnson. When Johnson pressed her to explain why, in the immediate aftermath, no one from the State Department had asked American evacuees if there had been a protest before the attack, Clinton replied:

In March 2013, Representative Duncan D. Hunter introduced legislation into the 113th Congress to authorize awarding of

Congressional Gold Medals to Doherty and Woods for their actions that led to their deaths.

In April 2013, the Pentagon announced the activation of a USMC quick response force for North Africa that would use the range and speed of the Bell Boeing V-22 Osprey to be able to respond to similar events in the future. Spain authorized the basing of the quick response force at Morón Air Base near Seville, for a temporary one-year term.

On May 13, 2013, President Obama stated during a news conference, "The day after it happened, I acknowledged that this was an act of terrorism." This claim was disputed by Glenn Kessler of The Washington Post in a "Fact Checker" article, which explored at length the difference in meaning between the phrases "act of terror" and "act of terrorism." In the article, Kessler accused Obama of "revisionist history" for stating he had called the attack an "act of terrorism" when it fact he had used the term "act of terror", observing that Obama had gone out of his way to avoid calling the incident an "act of terrorism" or blame the ambassador's death on terrorism.

On July 30, 2013 Rep. Ed Royce (R, CA-39) introduced the Department of State Operations and Embassy Security Authorization Act, Fiscal Year 2014 (H.R. 2848; 113th Congress). Supporters argued, "this bill advances efforts to improve the physical infrastructure at posts overseas to comply with the highest standards of protection; to increase training for those responsible for guarding our compounds and personnel; to put in place procedures that respond appropriately to threats, reducing the chances of another attack like that suffered in Benghazi, Libya; to review the policies and procedures of the Bureau of Diplomatic Security; to authorize the use of best value contracting at high risk, high threat posts; to authorize security improvements at soft targets; and to provide for security enhancements in line with Accountability Review Board recommendations."

Critics including Republican Party members accused the Obama White House and State Department of over-emphasizing or fabricating the role of Islamic anger over the anti-Islamic movie Innocence of Muslims and alleged that the administration was reluctant to label the attack as "terrorist". Representative Mike Rogers (R-MI), chairman of the House Intelligence Committee, who on September 13 said that the attacks had all the hallmarks of a coordinated attack by al-Qaeda, has questioned whether there were any protests at all in Benghazi, saying: "I have seen no information that shows that there was a protest going on as you have seen around any other embassy at the time. It was clearly designed to be an attack." According to critics, the consulate site should have been secured better both before and after the attack. GOP legislators also took issue with delays in the investigation, which CNN attributed to "bureaucratic infighting" between the FBI, Justice, and State. On September 26, Senator Johnny Isakson (R-Georgia) said he "cannot believe that the FBI is not on the ground yet".

Testimony from top U.S. commanders after the attack revealed that the military was unprepared for conflict across Africa and the Middle East. No attack aircraft had been placed on high alert on September 11, the anniversary of the September 11 attacks in 2001, and the closest fighter planes to trouble spots in North Africa were based in Aviano, Italy. The fighter planes based in Aviano were unarmed and no aerial refueling planes were within a 10-hour flight to the base. In addition, no AC-130 gunships were within a 10-hour flight of Libya, and their crews did not reach a staging base in Italy until 19 hours after the attack began.

With the attack and subsequent criticism occurring in the last two months of the 2012 U.S. Presidential election, Democrats and liberal media figures accused Republicans of politicizing the attacks in an unprecedented manner. Romney was accused by the Obama campaign of trying to exploit the attacks for political gain, leading the father of Ambassador Stevens to call for both campaigns to avoid making it a campaign issue.

Robert Gates, former CIA director and Defense Secretary under Republican Presidents and then President Obama until stepping down in July 2011, has said that some critics of the government's response have a "cartoonish" view of military capabilities. He stated that he would have responded with equal caution given the risks and the lack of intelligence on the ground, and that American forces require planning and preparation, which the circumstances did not allow for.

President Obama called the criticism a "sideshow" and later accused Congress of "taking its eye off the ball" on the subject of the economy and focusing on "phony scandals". White House Spokesman Jay Carney later specified that the criticism of the administration's handling of the Benghazi attacks was one of those "phony scandals".

On December 10, 2014, upon publication of the House Permanent Select Committee on Intelligence report on Benghazi, Committee Chairman Mike Rogers wrote in an op-ed piece, "The Obama administration's White House and State Department actions before, during, and after the Benghazi terrorist attack on September 11, 2012, ranged from incompetence to deplorable political manipulation in the midst of an election season."

The Center for Media and Public Affairs at George Mason University described the conclusions of an unpublished study on November 2, 2012. Based on a textual analysis that tallied the occurrence of certain words and phrases in news reports, the study concluded that leading newspapers in the U.S. framed the attack in terms of a spontaneous protest as framed by the Obama administration's version, four times as often as a planned terrorist attack, which was the Republican version.

Soon after the attack, Steve Kroft of CBS' 60 Minutes asked President Obama what he thought of the situation. The President avoided the question and would not call the event terrorism. The exchange was not released until days before the 2012 presidential elections. Journalist Bret Baier, host of Special Report with Bret Baier, noted "Obama would not say whether he thought the attack was terrorism. Yet he would later emphasize at a presidential debate that in the Rose Garden the same day, he had declared the attack an act of terror." Baier also states: "Two days before the election, CBS posted additional portions of a Sept. 12 '60 Minutes' interview where President Obama seems to contradict himself on the Benghazi attack."

Analyst Brit Hume said to CBS News that media bias is real in regards to Benghazi and if a Republican were president, there would have been much more critical and aggressive reporting. On September 13, progressive pundit Rachel Maddow, during her show on MSNBC, stated: "An organized attack. Anybody who tells you that what happened to our ambassador and our consulate in Libya was as a result of a protest over an offensive movie, you should ask them why they think that. That's the first version of events we heard. That does not seem to explain what happened that night or by the facts or the more facts we get." On June 2014, Maddow criticized the right-wing media for reporting an arrest as bad news, said that Americas are poorly served by the media, and that "the take on Fox News is that's not actually news" and now "they have to make it bad news, they have to make into maybe a scandal itself."

On the edition of October 24 of Fox News' Special Report with Bret Baier, syndicated columnist Charles Krauthammer claimed that a State Department e-mail, which passed along a report from Embassy Tripoli that Ansar al-Sharia had claimed responsibility for the attack on Facebook and Twitter, proved that the White House knew of terrorist connections to the attack almost immediately. Charles Krauthammer stated, "This is really a journalistic scandal. I mean, the fact there was not a word about any of this in the Times or the Post today."

Conservative pundit Jonah Goldberg of the National Review stated that on NBC's Meet the Press, host David Gregory changed the subject when a guest raised the subject of the Benghazi attack, saying, "Let's get to Libya a little bit later," but never returned to the subject.

On November 26, 2012, journalist Tom Ricks went on Fox News' Happening Now with Jon Scott to discuss the attack. While being interviewed on Fox News by Jon Scott, Ricks accused Fox News of being "extremely political" in its coverage of the attack and said that "Fox was operating as a wing of the Republican Party." Ricks accused the network of covering the story more than it needed to be. The interview was cut short and Ricks and the interview was not mentioned or covered by Fox News again. Fox News was subsequently criticized for cutting the interview short. In an interview with the Associated Press, Fox News' White House correspondent Ed Henry suggested that he thought Benghazi was being covered too much by the network. Henry said, "We've had the proper emphasis, but I would not be so deluded to say that some of our shows, some of our commentators, have covered it more than it needed to be covered."

A CNN/ORC poll published June 17, 2014 states that 61% of Americans are not satisfied with the Obama administration's handling of the situation, but are split 48% to 44% on whether Republicans have been too aggressive in the hearings.

Investigation

A number of official investigations have been completed, are ongoing, or are under consideration, with the United States House Select Committee on Benghazi's final report projected to be released in 2016. U.S. Representative Trey Gowdy (R.-S.C.), Chair of the committee, has cited a lack of cooperation from Obama administration officials and Secretary Clinton for the lack of progress.

FOIA requests

Freedom of Information Act requests have been made since the attack. The conservative foundation Judicial Watch filed a FOIA request to the Department of State on December 19, 2012. An acknowledgement of the request was received by Judicial Watch on January 4, 2013. When the State Department failed to respond to the request by February 4, 2013, Judicial Watch filed a lawsuit, which resulted in seven photographs being delivered on June 6, 2013. Three of the photographs show Arabic-language spray paint graffiti. According to preliminary translations provided to the U.K. MailOnline by the Investigative Project on Terrorism, the graffiti likely reads "Thrones of HamzaIn"; "Allah-u Akbar" ("God is Great"); and "Unity of ranks".

On May 30, 2013 it was reported that the Republican National Committee filed a FOIA for "any and all emails or other documents containing the terms 'Libya' and/or 'Benghazi' dated between September 11, 2012 and November 7, 2012 directed from or to U.S. Department of State employees originating from, or addressed to, persons whose email addresses end in either 'barackobama.com' or 'dnc.org'".

On April 18, 2014, the conservative group Judicial Watch released more than 100 pages of documents obtained through a FOIA lawsuit. One email, dated September 14, 2012, with a subject line "RE PREP CALL with Susan: Saturday at 4:00 pm ET", was from deputy national security advisor for strategic communications Rhodes stated: "Goals: ... To underscore that these protests are rooted in an Internet video, and not a broader failure of policy..." According to another e-mail obtained by Judicial Watch, when asked about whether the attack was linked to the Mohammad video, State Department spokesperson Victoria Nuland said she, "could not confirm a connect as we simply don't know—and we won't know until there is an investigation".

According to The Wall Street Journal, the e-mail was written to prepare U.S. Ambassador to the U.N. Susan Rice for her appearances on Sunday news shows two days later, and it "sets out the Administration's view of the cause of the Benghazi attacks". John Dickerson of Slate says the e-mail refers to the worldwide protests to Innocence of Muslims and not the Benghazi attack.